Puppy Training

The Ultimate Guide on How to Train Your Puppy to Become a Well Behaved Dog

By Vivaco Books

© Copyright 2014 – Vivaco Books

ISBN-13: 978-1530095421
ISBN-10: 1530095425

ALL RIGHTS RESERVED. No part of this publication may be reproduced or transmitted in any form whatsoever, electronic, or mechanical, including photocopying, recording, or by any informational storage or retrieval system without express written, dated and signed permission from the author.

Table of Contents

Introduction 1
   What This Book Is About 1

Chapter 1: How to Train a Puppy the Right Way 5
   Training Equipment 7
   Reward Training 9
   When Should You Start Training a Puppy? 9

Chapter 2: How to Teach Your Puppy to Come, Sit and Stay 13
   The 'COME' Command 14
   The 'SIT - STAY' Command 19

Chapter 3: How to Stop Your Puppy from Howling and Whining 27
   Day-to-Day Whining 30
   Demand or Excessive Barking and Whining 31
   Whining and Health Considerations 32

Chapter 4: How to Teach Your Puppy to Stop Jumping 33
   Jumping – A Continuous Problem 35
   Solving the Jumping Problem 35

Chapter 5: How to Stop Your Puppy from Begging 39

Teaching Him Not To Beg..40

Chapter 6: How to Properly Stop Excitement Urination...43

Conclusion..47

Introduction

What This Book Is About

This book contains all the necessary information that a new puppy owner should know throughout their puppy training journey. It is short and packed with practical information and steps you can follow, in order to train your puppy to become a well behaved dog.

In the first chapter, you will learn how to properly train your puppy the right way, using reward training. You will also find out when the right time is, to start training your puppy.

In Chapter 2, you will learn the importance of teaching the "Come" command to your dog. You will also get a set of simple training instructions, in order to properly teach this command to your puppy. Also, you will find out how to teach your dog to "Sit" and "Stay", using two different methods (Luring, Clicker), with proper step-by-step instructions.

In the third chapter, you will learn why puppies howl and whine and how to deal with such issues. You will then be able to determine the reason your puppy is whining, which could be from day-to-day whining, to excessive barking, to health related whining something you will have to identify as soon as possible and proceed accordingly.

In chapter 4, you will learn the reasons why puppies jump on people, why although it may seem harmless and cute, is actually a very unhealthy habit and can lead to serious problems. You will also be given step-by-step instructions, which will help you stop the jumping problem.

In the fifth chapter, you will learn why dogs beg in the first place (hint: it is not a natural behavior), find out how to stop your puppy from begging and even how to deal with exceptionally stubborn ones. In the last chapter, you will learn about excitement urination, if it is a habit that needs to be corrected or ignored and how to properly deal with such incidents once they happen.

Chapter 1: How to Train a Puppy the Right Way

The techniques and methods used for training puppies have seen a gradual change over the years. The modern training methods are not just good for your dog, but they are also easier and more comfortable for you. Most of the traditional training methods are adapted forms of the dog training given to military dogs. However, people fail to realize that military training focuses on the trait of dominance and is extremely brutal.

All the training methods used for military training of dogs focused, on extracting/eliminating bad behavior at early stages of the training process, to ensure that the same doesn't arise when it matters the most. Moreover, this type of training does not add any of the qualities to the dog's temperament that modern owner's desire. Therefore, to say the least, these methods are of minimal use in the present day scenario. With several new and more effective training methods present, the use of traditional training methods makes no sense.

Modern training methods like reward training and operant conditioning are based on the relationship between the stimulus given, response generated and the consequences of the response. Therefore, in a way, you are training the puppy by making him realize that his present action will determine what shall happen to him next. Now, the puppy doesn't perform an action out of fear of getting punished. Instead, he performs an action with the objective to get attention and affection.

While the traditional methods waited for the dog to commit a mistake and accordingly corrections were made using the leash method, the new method encourages the puppy to perform positive behavior on his own. As a result, the behavior is incorporated in his general behavior and is no more a pushed and positioned action. All in all, the focus of any training should be on training that is not just efficient and effective, but also enjoyable and easy.

Training Equipment

The modern training methodology has been incorporated in several training tools as well. Some of these newest tools are the easy walk harness, which communicates with the puppy in a natural fashion to stop him from lunging forward and jumping, and head halters, which fit over the head of the dog and allow easy control over the most massive sized dogs.

Besides these, several different types of collars are also available. The conventional choke collar fits well on the dog's neck and the jerk action of the same can be easily used to direct the actions of the dog. However, if not put appropriately, you can hurt the dog as the pressure may be applied, but it may not be released. These injuries can be all the more profound if you have a small sized dog. In fact, you may cause collapsed trachea or permanent damage to the neck. Therefore, its use requires proper knowledge, so as to not cause any injuries on your dog.

Another type of collars available on the market is electronic collars, which impart a low intensity electric shock to the dog and can be controlled using a remote. Their use is extremely controversial, and only professional trainers must use it for training purposes.

Reward Training

There are several other training methods that link, verbal commands to actions or use sound signals, rewards or clicker to derive positive behavior. Regardless of the method used, the most vital part of the training process is to teach the puppy how and why to comply with the instructions. For instance, if you want to teach your puppy to 'sit', to actually perform the action is 5% of the job. The rest 95% is to make the puppy understand why he should sit.

When Should You Start Training a Puppy?

Puppies are similar to sponges and possess a good absorbing capacity. They are exceptionally good learners, and they start learning from the very first minute they enter your home. Once your puppy has attained the age of 6-8 weeks, you can expect him to start learning basic commands. However, some puppies may be quicker at learning commands than others. Therefore, no generalization can be made in this regard.

An important thing to remember while training your puppies is to avoid using the word 'no'. If you use the word 'no' too often, your puppy may start believing that 'no' is his name. Training is a process of learning and mistakes are an integral part of that learning process. On the other hand, you must use the word 'yes' as much as possible. In fact, use the word 'yes' as and when the opportunity arises. This is the way your puppy will know, what you want him to do on a regular basis.

However, you may argue that pointing out mistakes is equally important. However, instead of shouting out the word 'no', you must look for methods and techniques that can be used to correct negative behavior in a manner that you encourage a positive behavior. Also, make it a point to reward the puppy whenever he performs positive behavior.

Lastly, it is important for you to realize that puppies do not have a long attention span. Therefore, it is good to plan small, but frequent training sessions instead of going for the kill in one long session. Besides this, setting up a schedule and following a routine are equally crucial. This is the best way to know how eager your dog is towards training routines.

Training sessions involve extensive use of rewards and treats. Therefore, the best time for training is right before meals, as the puppy's nutrition and food intake will remain balanced. In addition, if you plan your training sessions before meals, you can be sure that your puppy is going to be more eager for his treats, rather than some time after his meal, which by then he will be probably full.

Chapter 2: How to Teach Your Puppy to Come, Sit and Stay

Come, sit and stay are the three most basic commands in puppy training. You will definitely have a more pleasurable interaction with your dog, once you realize he is able to follow your commands and obey you.

The 'COME' Command

The first of this set of commands is 'come'. Knowing and following these commands is not just a sign of polite behavior, but it can be also a life-saving command in many situations. If left unsupervised, some puppies, especially the more curious ones, can get into trouble. Even if you watch your puppy all the time, a squirrel can tempt the puppy to run into traffic.

In such a scenario, if your puppy recognizes and obeys the command, come, you can call him from a distance and save him from possible troubles or even injuries. If you have been around a puppy, you will know that puppies can be very quick, and sometimes, it may be impossible to catch them. Therefore, the only way you can get the puppy to come to you is by using the 'come' command. This command shall allow you to keep your puppy within reach without using a leash or any other form of control.

Before moving any further, it is important to mention the most common mistakes that owners commit, when they attempt to teach this command to their puppies. If your puppy is not following the 'come' command, then there may be several reasons. Young puppies do not even recognize their names. Therefore, expecting them to know a command may be too much from them.

In the majority of the cases, a puppy doesn't respond to a command because he does not know what the command means. Your puppy will be able to relate the command with an action only after you explain the relation to him in his language.

Will you be able to follow instructions in a language you do not know? The answer is obviously no.

The same rule applies to puppies. They will never be able to understand your instructions unless you illustrate them in their language. However, after you have interacted with the puppy for some time, they will start understanding your language as well and communication will become easier.

If the dog recognizes the command and still doesn't obey it, then you can assume that the command holds no significance to the puppy. In other words, the puppy does not feel that the command is of any benefit to him. Why should the puppy leave a butterfly or a ball for you? This brings us to another important facet of puppy training. You must look for alternate behaviors that are more inviting to your puppy and compel him to behave in a manner that you like.

The biggest mistake in puppy training, which is also the most common one, is punishing the dog for bad behavior. The fact that he is not abiding by your instructions may bother you, but you will have to hold your horses and show some patience. Regardless of how upset and annoyed you may be with the disobedient behavior, you cannot afford to shout at your puppy.

When you punish them, they learn that they will be punished when they come back to you, which encourages negative behavior.

Training Instructions for Teaching 'Come' –

#1: The first thing to figure out before you start the training process, is to look for the reward that your puppy likes the most. A perfect treat is one that is tempting and pure irresistible for the puppy. Also, treats should be small and aromatic and should not be large enough to fill your puppy's stomach and become a substitute for food.

#2: Always choose a time when there are minimal distractions. For instance, you can choose a time when your kids are not around, or your other pets are taking a nap. The chances of getting the puppy's attention at this time are greater than other times.

#3: Once you have been able to get the puppy's attention, call out 'come' along with his name. Then run in the opposite direction and repeat the same step. The puppy will be compelled to chase you as dogs have a natural affiliation to social play.

#4: Let him come to you and catch you. Every time he is able to do this successfully, reward him with a treat and shower him with praises. Petting and rewards are signals to the puppy that you like his actions and behavior. He will be urged to repeat this behavior in order to please you.

#5: Perform this chase a few times. However, do not overdo it and stop before your puppy begins to show disinterest in the game.

#6: Once you have practiced this command for almost a week, try to practice the command while standing still. Just show a treat to your puppy and call out the combination of name and come command. However, be sure not to practice the command when the puppy is eating or sleepy.

#7: If your puppy has started recognizing the command, then you can give this command to the puppy while he is doing some activity like chasing a ball. Also, practice that command at locations other than your backyard or inside of your home.

#8: Reward and praise your puppy every single time that he comes to you. You want the puppy to relate 'coming to you' with positive things. This is the secret of getting this command right.

The 'SIT - STAY' Command

The 'come' command can be used in isolation or in conjunction with the 'sit-stay' command. Like the 'come' command, the 'sit-stay' command is also a command that adds politeness to the behavior of the dog. Moreover, it can also be used in isolation for target behaviors like when you open a door or as a way to thank you for giving them food. Some puppies are extremely high on energy and planting the tail can help you in keeping them under control.

Puppies are quick learners, and like everything else, they learn to game the system just as quickly. They may sit for a moment and bounce up at the very sight of a ball or a squirrel. In order to keep them planted in their position, it is essential to couple the 'sit' command with a 'stay' command. Therefore, a 'sit' and 'stay' combination keeps the dog in place and increases the time of contact between his butt and the floor.

The first step of teaching this combination is to teach the 'sit' command. You can teach the 'sit' command using two methods namely, the luring method and the clicker method. The luring method makes use of treats to gain the puppy's attention while the clicker method uses the clicker training tool, for training the puppy.

The Luring Method for Teaching 'SIT'

The luring method requires you to follow these steps —

#1: Take a few treats handy with you. However, ensure that they are not visible to the puppy.

#2: Stand right in front of the puppy and speak command 'sit' using a firm and clear voice.

#3: Take a treat in your hand and hold it right in front of his nose. Once the puppy has started following the treat with movements of his head, move your hand in the upward direction, towards the head of the puppy. Raising the head disturbs his balance and he is forced to sit.

#4: As soon as the puppy goes into the 'sit' position, give him the treat.

This exercise must be repeated several times a day, in short training sessions. Once the puppy starts following your command, practice it in another location and setting. You can also change the hand signal to a closed fist. Either case, always be sure to reward the puppy with a treat every time the correct action is performed.

The Clicker Method for Teaching 'SIT

Clicker training is different from the luring method in the sense that it focuses on altering the natural behavior of the puppy. Therefore, training using this method may take longer, but it will also be permanent.

The steps for this method are the following –

#1: Keep a few treats and a clicker handy.

#2: Wait for the puppy to sit and click whenever he performs this action. Accompany the click with a treat. Therefore, the click tells him that you like this behavior, and the treat reinforces the behavior. The puppy may not be able to figure it out initially, but after the click-treat pattern is repeated a couple of times, he will know the pattern.

#3: Once the puppy has recognized what caused the click and treat, associate the action with a command. Whenever you click the clicker, say out the word, 'sit'. Practice this command several times a day and once the dog has got used to this command, you can practice it at different locations.

As your puppy practices this command, he will get comfortable with it, and it will become a part of his behavior. Now that your puppy has learned the 'sit' command, you just have to teach him to elongate the duration of sitting and the command becomes 'sit-stay'.

Here are a set of instructions that can be used for this purpose –

#1: Keep treats handy and choose a place where there are minimal distractions.

#2: Start with the 'sit' command and once the puppy sits, say 'stay' and give him a treat.

#3: Set your first goal at 10 seconds and give the puppy a treat after saying the word stay repeatedly, every 3 to 4 seconds. After the 10 second period is over, you can release him by saying, 'okay' and clicking if you are using a clicker for training. Also, give him a treat, but this treat should be smaller than the treat that you give for staying. If the puppy gets up before the 10 second period, do not give him any treat.

$4: After a few rounds, your puppy will figure out the rules of the game. Once you realize that your puppy has got the trick, practice the command with him several times a day in short training sessions.

#5: Now that your puppy is a master of the '10 second sit-stay', you can increase the time and practice as mentioned above.

#6: When his time of stay has reached as high as 80 seconds, increase the time between treats by a few seconds with the target to reach a treat-less session. This is a major milestone as far as this command is concerned.

If you are confident that your puppy has learned the 'sit-stay' command, practice it while standing at a distance from the puppy. Gradually, increase the distance from a few steps to across the room, a few steps at a time. In such a way, the treats will no longer be visible, and the puppy will be able to take commands without the treat.

In most obedience trials, sit-stay command compliance is tested. In fact, novices are known to hold a sit-stay for only as long as one minute. On the other hand, trained dogs may stay in their sit position for longer and follow your command even if you are standing at a distance from them. Therefore, the longer the dog is able to stay in the 'sit' position and take the command from a distance, the better trained he is for obedience.

Chapter 3: How to Stop Your Puppy from Howling and Whining

Dogs are family pets, and they love to be surrounded by their family members all the time. As a result, they easily succumb to conditions like separation anxiety. Two of the primary byproducts of separation anxiety are whining and howling. This is particularly the case when your puppy is left for the very first time. Basically, the puppy senses danger and howls and whines to send out an alarm to you that he is alone and unprotected.

You will mostly notice this behavior when the puppy is newly put in a crate or confined. However, you must understand that this behavior is perfectly normal. In some cases, the crying may become so profound and loud that you may start getting worried about the wellbeing of your puppy. As a rule, every puppy cries out loud when he is placed inside the crate.

In order to stop the puppy from excessive whining and howling, you can do the following –

Be proactive in your approach and help the puppy to accept privacy and isolation. This will reduce the effects of separation anxiety.

\# If the puppy whines and cries when left inside the crate, do not rush back to him immediately. Wait for the time when the puppy pauses his whining and take him out during that period.

\# Do not crate him for long periods of time. This is a new area for the puppy and it will take him some time to acclimatize to that environment. Leave him inside for some time and then take him around for a while before putting him inside again.

\# If your puppy refuses to stay inside the crate, put a treat or a toy to tempt him. Firstly, this will entice him to enter the crate and stay there. Besides this, it will also give him something to pass his time inside the crate. Therefore, he will not whine or cry out of boredom.

Whining and crying may not always be non-indicative. Sometimes, they may be indications of an issue or problem. It may be your puppy's way telling you that he is facing issues. The puppy may not be comfortable inside the crate because of the following reasons –

It may be too hot or cold inside.

The space may be too small for the puppy to accommodate.

You must address these issues on priority basis and make the puppy feel comfortable inside the crate before implementing any training method.

Day-to-Day Whining

We believe that dogs whine for no reason. However, this may not always be the case. Sometimes, a dog may whine because his ball has got stuck somewhere or he is calling his playmate. In these cases, whining is acceptable.

However, if it goes beyond tolerable limits, it should be reprimanded and stopped. Be sure to look for the issue and solve it before switching to a reprimanding mode.

Demand or Excessive Barking and Whining

In some cases, dogs turn to whining and crying because they know that this will get them instant attention from you. This behavioral pattern is also called demand whining. However, if a dog is allowed to whine for demands, it soon transforms into a habit. If this is the case with your dog, you can overcome the problem by fulfilling your puppy's demands to the extent that he does not have anything to cry for.

You can start by giving sufficient food and attention to the puppy. If he begins to demand either by whining or crying, simply ignore him and his demands. By fulfilling his demands in this manner, you encourage him to pursue this behavior as a habit. In addition to this, teaching the puppy to follow a command like, 'Stop Crying', can be helpful in getting momentary relief from excessive barking or whining.

Whining and Health Considerations

If your dog has not been whining as a rule and all of a sudden he starts doing so, it may be his way of telling you that something is wrong. Therefore, you must consider taking him to the vet for a quick checkup.

Chapter 4: How to Teach Your Puppy to Stop Jumping

Which is the scariest and the most annoying action of pet dogs? When asked this question, a majority of people shall answer, 'jumping'.

Do you know why dogs jump on people? They have no negative intentions. In fact, it is just their way to greet people. Dogs are social animals and actions like bouncing, leaping and jumping are a puppy's ways to attract attention.

You must have noticed the fact that many people pet their puppies by sitting with them on the ground and allowing them to wriggle up to their face. This seems to be perfectly fine when you are at the ground level with them.

However, you must discourage the dog from doing this when you are standing or sitting on a chair. Indulging in such activities tells your puppy that you approve of his jumping. Moreover, you may approve of the behavior when the puppy is young, but it is sure to get problematic as the puppy grows. So, what was cute once will become dangerous in the long run.

Jumping – A Continuous Problem

The fundamental reason why this habit of jumping grows with the puppy is our inconsistency. When the puppy jumps on you randomly, you either ignore it or give him the attention he demands. Therefore, the puppy classifies jumping as a good behavior.

On the other hand, if the puppy jumps on you when you are dressed up for a party, you get annoyed and punish him. This punishment is also seen by him as praise because he is getting what he wants, your attention. However, if you punish him severely, he may stop jumping on you, but the problem shall continue to exist. Now, although he may stop jumping on you, he will still jump on other people.

Solving the Jumping Problem

The basic principle of puppy training is that the only way you can prevent a dog from repeating negative behavior is to teach him an alternate behavior for the situation. As mentioned previously, jumping is a dog's way to greet people. Therefore, if you are able to teach him another way of saying hello to people, he will stop jumping. For instance, you can teach your dog to sit down and stay at his position. Once the dog follows your command, you can pet him and shower him with love and praises.

In order to ensure that the jumping problem is solved in its entirety, you must follow a few but at the same time important instructions –

#1: Be consistent

#2: Interrupt and correct his behavior if he jumps on someone else. Following the 'stop jumping' technique on a personal basis will not solve your problem. If you want to get rid of the jumping problem in its entirety, you must ensure that no one in your family or friend circle allows the puppy to jump on them. If any of your friends or members of your family intervene and let the dog jump on them, interrupt it there and then and correct the dog's behavior.

#3: Give him attention and affection when he performs good behavior

#4: Discourage negative behavior by ignorance

#5: Practice is the key to success. Be persistent in your efforts and practice an alternative behavior on a daily basis so that it gets included in the general behavior of the puppy. Even if it requires you going out the back door and coming back in through the front door, do it several times a day to give your puppy the necessary practice.

#6: Remember that the dog is particularly excited to see you come home, and he may not take the sit-stay command seriously if you have not practiced the command with him in normal situations. Therefore, teach the sit-stay command before incorporating it in this process.

Lastly, it is beneficial to realize that jumping can be particularly dangerous, in addition to being scary and annoying. Elderly people and young children can easily get traumatized by a huge dog jumping on them. This can lead to accidents.

In addition to causing injury to others, they may also harm their own selves in the process. Therefore, it is important to teach your puppy not to jump in his early life and therefore preventing it from becoming a serious problem in his adult life.

Chapter 5: How to Stop Your Puppy from Begging

Although begging as a behavioral pattern is harmless, it is certainly one of the most irritating behaviors. Everyone wants to have an undistracted and relaxed meal and a drooling dog can be extremely uncomfortable.

Before going any further, it is necessary to understand why dogs beg. Begging is not a natural or inherited behavioral pattern. In fact, it is one of those behaviors that are learnt by your puppy and you may have, unintentionally, played a significant role in the process.

A puppy picks up the begging behavior when you slip something from your dinner plate and give it to him. It you do this a couple of times, then it will not take long before you see the dog standing beside your dining chair and expecting some food from your plate. When you succumb to his demands, you teach him to ask for more food, encouraging the begging behavior. This is how you unintentionally teach your puppy to beg.

Teaching Him Not To Beg

As soon as the puppy arrives at your home, ensure that you set up an eating schedule for the dog. Moreover, the eating schedule should be set so that your dinner time is his rest, sleep or eating time. As a rule, the puppy should not be around when you are eating your meal.

However, if your dog has already picked up the habit, then it will require a lot of patience and persistence on your part to help your puppy break this bad habit. The rule is simple – Don't give him any food! Remember the 'reward and praise' principle of training. Whenever you give the puppy something to eat or a treat, he assumes that you are happy with his behavior. Therefore, when you succumb to his begging and give him food, you are telling him that you are in agreement with that particular behavior.

Also, your dog might get to know that a little crying and whining can earn him even more treats. So, you simply have to refrain yourself from accepting any unreasonable demands of your puppy.

Here are a few tips that you can use to deal with stubborn puppies –

#1: Keep the puppy away during your meal time. You can either crate him or keep him in another area of the house.

#2: Schedule his meals in congruence with your meal times. Therefore, if he has his food in bowl, he is not as likely to come to you for food.

The main objective here is to keep the puppy out of sight, to avoid getting into a situation where you or a member of your family, gives food to your puppy from their own plate. Negative reinforcement is the best method to stop a dog from repeating the begging behavior. In fact, this method is known to be effective for extremely stubborn dogs as well.

Chapter 6: How to Properly Stop Excitement Urination

Your puppy may have been impeccable at house training, but you may notice him leaving a puddle of urine, when he comes to greet you. This is exactly what excitement urination means. Besides this, it is crucial for you to know that excitement urination is absolutely normal for small puppies and does not indicate any abnormality or condition.

Excitement urination is commonly observed in puppies because they have little control over their bladders. When a puppy urinates out of excitement, he does not know that he is urinating. Therefore, if you punish the dog for this action, then it will only confuse him. Since the puppy is unaware of the reason for your anger, his excitement urination will become submissive urination.

The problem will be resolved on its own as the puppy grows and achieves control over his bladder. Therefore, the best management technique to sail through this period is to do everything possible for keeping the puppy dry. If the puppy does not get excited, then he will not exhibit excitement urination. It is as simple as that!

So, how can you prevent the puppy from getting excited by a stimulus?

In order to explain this, take the example of a joke that you have just heard. The first time you hear a joke, you laugh aloud at it. However, if the joke is repeated, it will not amuse you as much as it did the first time. Likewise, a stimulus may excite a puppy the first few times, but if the puppy is exposed to the stimulus repeatedly, the puppy will get used to that stimulus and will not get excited by it.

Also, you will notice that a puppy wets due to this reason mostly when you return home. As and when you notice this action, ignore the puppy to tell him that you dislike this behavior. The rule of thumb here is to ignore excitement urination and never punish the dog for it. All you need is a little patience and persistence. Keep your focus intact and continue your efforts to train your puppy to become a well behaved dog with full rigor and enthusiasm.

Conclusion

The next step is to apply what you have learned and put everything into action. We will be more than happy to learn how this book has helped you in yours and your dog's life and the progress that you have made.

If you feel you have learned something or you think it offered you some value, please take a moment to leave an honest review on Amazon. It would help many future readers who will be forever grateful to you. As we will!

With Best Regards,

Vivaco Books

ALL RIGHTS RESERVED. No part of this publication may be reproduced or transmitted in any form whatsoever, electronic, or mechanical, including photocopying, recording, or by any informational storage or retrieval system without express written, dated and signed permission from the author.

DISCLAIMER AND/OR LEGAL NOTICES: Every effort has been made to accurately represent this book and it's potential. Results vary with every individual, and your results may or may not be different from those depicted. No promises, guarantees or warranties, whether stated or implied, have been made that you will produce any specific result from this book. Your efforts are individual and unique, and may vary from those shown. Your success depends on your efforts, background and motivation.

The material in this publication is provided for educational and informational purposes. Use of the programs, advice, and information contained in this book is at the sole choice and risk of the reader.

Printed in Poland
by Amazon Fulfillment
Poland Sp. z o.o., Wrocław